Miss Jessie
Missionary Nurse in China

Miss Jessie
Missionary Nurse in China

Beth Branyon

PROVIDENCE HOUSE PUBLISHERS
Franklin, Tennessee

To the memory of Eloise Glass Cauthen whose deep love for Jessie Pettigrew Glass was the inspiration for this book.

Copyright 1996 by Beth Branyon

All rights reserved. Written permission must be secured from the publisher to use or reproduce any part of this book, except for brief quotations in critical reviews and articles.

Printed in the United States of America

ISBN: 1-881576-77-9

Cover design and illustrations by:
Schwalb Creative Communications, Inc.; photographs provided courtesy of Beth Branyon, the Foreign Mission Board, Southern Baptist Convention, Woman's Missionary Union, Southern Baptist Convention, Archives, and the Cauthen family.

PROVIDENCE HOUSE PUBLISHERS
238 Seaboard Lane • Franklin, Tennessee 37067
800-881-5692

Miss Jessie's home in Fincastle, Virginia.

Mrs. Pettigrew was pouring the water into the glasses. Twenty-year-old Jessie came through the door. She stopped and put her bonnet on the peg beside the door. She shook the dust from her long, blue skirt. All the horses in the streets of Fincastle, Virginia, made the streets very dusty.

"Jessie, you're late coming home from mission meeting. Supper is already on the table. Did everything go well today?" Mrs. Pettigrew asked.

"Oh, yes," Jessie said. "There were three ladies at the meeting. They gave thirty cents for missions. We read the letter from Miss Lottie Moon. She wrote that she needs women to help her with her work in China. I feel that God is calling me to become a missionary. I wish I could go to China like Miss Moon."

Jessie sat down beside her father. He looked at her and said softly, "Jessie, I am sure God does not want you to leave your family and go to that strange land of China. You can do just as much good work here in Fincastle. You can lead your women's mission group and raise money to send to the missionaries. Besides, your mother needs you to help her with her little Sunbeam mission group."

"Oh, father, I just feel I should be doing more mission work. Just think, if I could go to China. . . ."

Mr. Pettigrew said loudly, "Jessie, I won't listen to another word about your going away to China. I've heard that some Chinese do not want missionaries to come to their country. These Chinese have even killed some of the missionaries. This talk about becoming a missionary to China has to stop!"

"But father . . . ," Jessie cried.

Her father stopped her. "Jessie, I know you are old enough to leave home. I will let you go and live with your uncle and brothers in Louisiana. I think you will see how hard it is to be away from your family. Maybe then you will give up this idea of going to the other side of the world."

Jessie hugged her father. "Oh, Father, I will try to get a job to pay for my room and meals. I will make you proud of me."

When Jessie got to Louisiana, her uncle told her of the Touro Infirmary in New Orleans. It was a school where she could study nursing. Maybe after she finished school, she could get a job as a nurse.

Jessie wanted to go there. She had to use her money to buy the three dresses, twelve aprons, six white collars, black shoes, watch, and scissors which every nurse had to have.

Jessie wrote her family and told them about studying to be a nurse. Her father wrote back that he was happy she was thinking of becoming a nurse. What he did not know was that she was still dreaming of becoming a missionary.

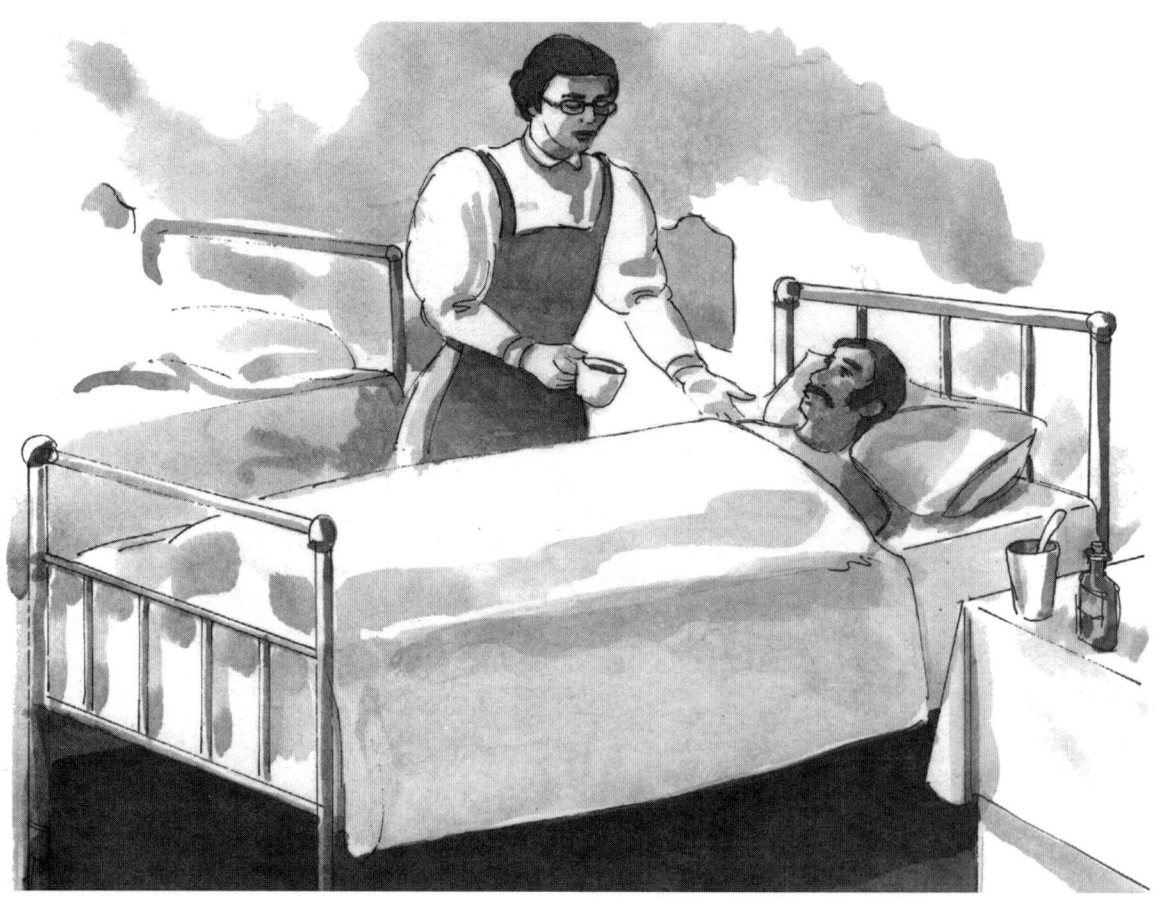

Jessie's church in New Orleans was Coliseum Place Baptist Church.

After Jessie finished nursing school in 1899, she went to work as a nurse in New Orleans. Even though she was very busy, she went to Sunday School, worship services, and other church activities.

Jessie never gave up her idea of becoming a missionary. When the Baptists met in New Orleans, she met Dr. R. J. Willingham, who was the Foreign Mission Board president. Later she wrote to see if the board were going to send any more missionaries to China. She prayed as she waited for the answer.

Dear Miss Pettigrew,

Thank you for your letter about going to China. I must tell you that it is hard to be a missionary in China. You must learn how to speak Chinese and write with a brush and ink. You must begin to eat with chopsticks. You will need to eat the foods which the people eat, like noodles. You will need to ride a donkey. Most of the time, you will walk. At times you will have to sleep on a hard bed with no mattress. Even if you have a mattress, it may be filled with corn shucks. Often you will have to put a net around your bed to keep out the mosquitoes.

Some people will not want you to be in China. They will call you a "foreign devil." You will miss your family. You can only come home about every seven to ten years.

The Foreign Mission Board does not have any money now to send another missionary to China. We will write you if we are going to send someone.

Your friend in Christ,
Dr. R. J. Willingham

One day, Jessie heard that a missionary doctor was being sent to China. If a doctor was going, the Foreign Mission Board might want to send a nurse. She wrote another letter to the Foreign Mission Board. Soon she got an answer to her letter.

> *Dear Miss Pettigrew,*
>
> *Thank you for your letter. Your information is right. The Foreign Mission Board is going to send a doctor to China. Dr. T. W. Ayers is going to work in Shandong Province, China. We hear that the Chinese women will not let a man help them even when they are sick. We will need to send a nurse to work with the women and to help Dr. Ayers. We hope to send the nurse when we have the money.*
>
> *If we decide to send a nurse to China, we will write you.*
>
> *Your friend in Christ,*
> *Dr. R. J. Willingham*

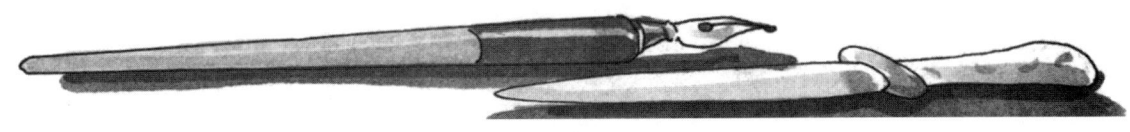

Many people wanted Jessie to go to China. They sent letters to the Foreign Mission Board. They said that she was one of the best nurses in New Orleans. They said she was a hard worker. Her church wrote that she had a very strong faith.

Jessie prayed and prayed. One day, a letter came from the Foreign Mission Board.

Dear Miss Pettigrew,

We are happy to tell you that you will be the first woman appointed by the Foreign Mission Board to be a nurse. You will work with Dr. T. W. Ayers and the other missionaries in China. When you get there, you will stay with Miss Lottie Moon while you study Chinese and learn about life in China.

Please come to Richmond, Virginia, so we can meet you. You can then go to visit your family in Fincastle. We also want you to go to Chicago to study more about the Bible. Then you will go to San Francisco to get a boat to go to China. The trip on the boat will take about one month.

Let me know when you can come to Richmond. We are glad you are going to serve Jesus Christ in China.

Your friend in Christ,
Dr. R. J. Willingham

Jessie sailed to China on December 23, 1901, when she was twenty-four years old. One of the people on the boat was Miss Hartwell whose family had been missionaries in China for many years. She told Jessie many stories about China.

When Jessie arrived in Chefoo, China, she had to travel by *shentze* to the house at the Little Cross Roads where Miss Lottie Moon lived. A *shentze* was like a big basket turned on its side which rode on poles between two mules.

Finally, Jessie arrived at Miss Moon's house in Tengchow. She was surprised to find Miss

Miss Lottie Moon agreed to have her picture made with Miss Jeter (left) and Jessie (right) in 1907. (Courtesy—Woman's Missionary Union, Southern Baptist Convention, Archives.)

Moon dressed in a Chinese robe over her long American skirt. "*Huan ying, huan ying*!" Miss Lottie cried. "That means 'welcome' in Chinese. I am so glad to see you, Jessie. I have been waiting for 'my little Virginia girl.' I have made some of my cookies just for you. We can eat while we talk. I hope you have brought news from my family and friends in Virginia. I miss them so much. It has been so many years since I have seen them."

"Yes, of course, I have many, many letters for you," Jessie replied. "Oh, Miss Moon. I cannot believe I am here in China. I believe God has always planned for me to serve him here. I just wish that

my father had not been so sad to see me leave."

"Well," Miss Lottie said, "we will pray that some day your father will be as happy about your being in China as we are to have you here. There is so much work to be done. I know you will spend most of your time helping Dr. Ayers. I hope you will have time to go with me to the villages to tell the women the Bible stories."

"Oh, Miss Moon, I want to do as much as I can to tell the people about Jesus."

"Well," Miss Moon responded, "first you must learn to speak and write Chinese. I will let you rest, but we have much work to do."

Soon, the Chinese lessons started. Jessie's teacher was a man with a pigtail which went almost to his feet. He had on a blue gown with a black jacket. Out from one of his sleeves, the teacher took a book with Chinese words in it. Out from the other sleeve, he took a Chinese brush and an ink stick. For Jessie, "Chinese school" had started.

Jessie had to learn how to make ink by rubbing the ink stick in water. She had to learn how to

make the Chinese "picture words" using a brush and the ink. She also had to learn how to say the words she wrote. Jessie was so proud when she learned to count to ten in Chinese.

Jessie learned to love Miss Moon when she stayed at her home. Miss Moon was so kind to her. When Miss Moon went home to Virginia, she went to Fincastle to visit Jessie's parents. She told them about Jessie and her work. Jessie's father was proud of his daughter. He was glad

she was safe and happy in China.

    Jessie did not stay with Miss Moon very long. She soon moved into the house built for Dr. Ayers and his family, but Miss Moon was always special to Jessie. Later, when Miss Moon got sick, she asked if Jessie could come and take care of her. Miss Moon was so ill that she was put on a ship to come home to America. Jessie was very sad when she was told that Miss Moon had died on the way back to her home in Virginia.

Women of China often had bound feet.

Jessie continued her work as a nurse. Sometimes, she would ride in a *shentze* out into the countryside to see the poor women. Today, Jessie was riding in a sedan chair which was carried by two men. The men were servants of a rich Chinese woman Jessie had gone to see.

At first, only the poor people would allow the foreign doctors and nurses to help them. Now even many of the rich Chinese were willing to invite the missionaries to their homes.

The rich Chinese woman, Li Tai Tai, could not come to the hospital because she had "bound" feet. As a baby, her feet had been bound, or tied, so they could not grow. Now, her feet were only four inches long. The Chinese thought small feet were very pretty. Li Tai Tai could not walk very well. When she needed to go somewhere, she had to be carried by her servants. When she wanted to see someone, the person had to come to her.

Li Tai Tai had become sick with a fever. She would not allow Dr. Ayers to help her because he was a man. She had heard that the missionary hospital had a woman who would come and visit you if you were sick. She had sent her servants to the hospital to get Jessie. Jessie had gone to see Li Tai Tai and had returned to the hospital to

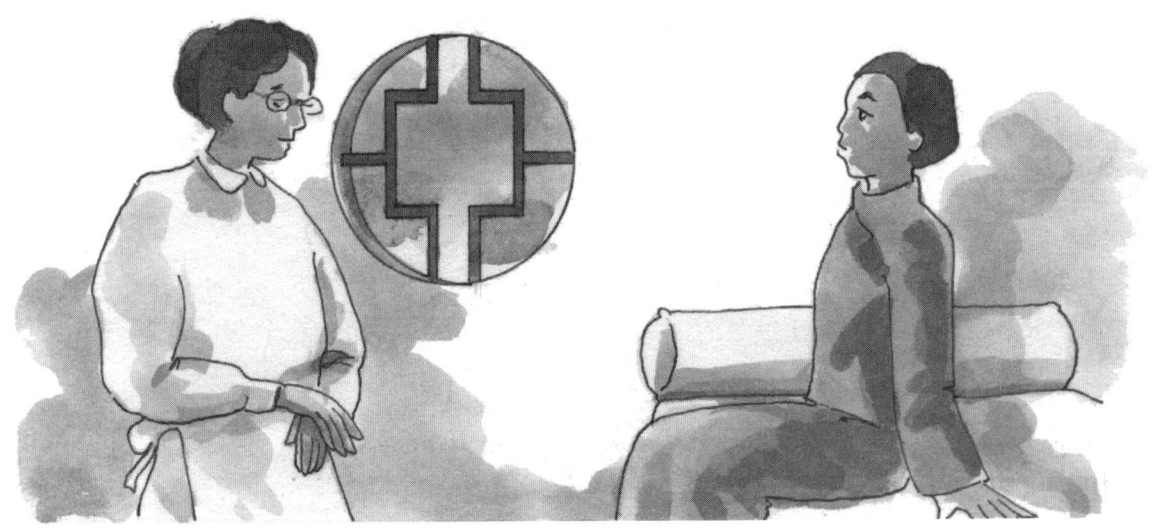

get some medicine to help her get well.

The servants put the sedan chair down at the gate of the hospital. "Miss Jessie," Dr. Ayers said, "I am so glad you are back. I need you to help me with an operation. They have just brought a man to the hospital with a badly broken leg."

As they walked, Dr. Ayers asked Jessie if the visit to Li Tai Tai had been a good visit. "Yes," she replied. "I was able to tell her about Jesus. She had never heard about him. I love being able to help people who are sick, but I love even more telling them about Jesus being God's Son."

"You know," Dr. Ayers said, "more and more people are hearing about Jesus. We are seeing more churches being started. Now even Chinese young men are starting to become preachers. We have many reasons to thank God."

Jessie and Dr. Ayers went inside the hospital. "I just wish," Jessie said, "that I had more time to go out to the small towns and into the homes to talk with the women about Jesus. I wish we had more help here at the hospital. There are so many people who are sick. If people would give more money for missions, more people could come to China as missionaries."

Mr. Glass with Eloise (left), Bentley, and Lois.

Jessie was busy all of the time. She worked hard taking care of the Chinese people who were sick. She was also the nurse for all of the missionary families.

One of the American missionaries, Mrs. Eunice Glass, became very sick. Jessie went to her house every day to take care of her, but Mrs. Glass was so sick that she died. Now, Mr. Wiley Glass, his son, Bentley, and his two daughters, Lois and Eloise, were alone. It was really hard for the girls because Lois was just seven, and Eloise was only five.

After Mrs. Glass died, Jessie still walked over from the hospital to see the children. She was so kind to them that they grew to love her. Wiley Glass also began to love Jessie.

After some time, Wiley asked Jessie to marry him. "You know, Jessie," he said, "my family has learned to love you. It is hard for the children to be here in China without a mother. Would you like to be my wife and their mother?"

"Oh, Wiley, I love you and your family, but I am a nurse. If I married you, I would have to stop working at the hospital. It would take all of my time to take care of you and the children. The Chinese people need me. I will have to pray and find out what God wants me to do."

Mr. Glass in his study.

Jessie wanted to marry Wiley. Some of the missionaries wanted her to marry him, but others wanted her to continue being a nurse. Jessie did not know what to do. She could not make up her mind while she was in China. It was almost time for her to go home to America to visit. She left China without saying goodbye to Wiley or his family.

"God, what should I do?" she prayed. "I love Wiley and his family. Should I marry him? The children need a mother."

Finally, she decided to marry him. She sent Wiley a telegram saying she was sorry she had left him. Would he forgive her? He sent her a telegram back. It only had one word—"Forgiven." Now Jessie was sure God wanted her to marry Wiley—and soon.

Jessie's wedding picture. (Courtesy—Foreign Mission Board, Southern Baptist Convention.)

Jessie was so happy. She was on a train going west to get a boat to go to Japan. Wiley was going to go to Japan from China and meet her. They were going to be married in Japan and then go home to China.

Everything seemed to go wrong! The train was in a snowstorm and could not move for four days. When she got to the dock, the boat had sailed. Now she was alone in a hotel room with no money to buy another ticket. What could she do? Wiley would be in Japan, and she would still be in America. Jessie was sad.

"Dear God," Jessie prayed, "I know you want me to marry Wiley. Please help me find a way to get to Japan."

God answered her prayer. A letter came from the Foreign Mission Board. Someone had read about the train, and knew she was on it. The mission board had decided to send her salary for the next four months. It was enough to buy a new ticket.

When she got to Japan, Wiley was there. They were married in 1916 when she was thirty-eight. They soon went back to China. Their first visit was to the school where Bentley, Lois, and Eloise lived. Miss Jessie had brought dolls for the girls and a basketball for Bentley.

The children ran to her. "Oh, we are so happy that you are finally here and going to be our mother."

"I thank God for giving me such a wonderful family," Jessie said.

Later, Jessie gave birth to two other children. One was a girl named Gertrude, whom everyone called "Trudy." The other was a boy named Bryan.

As the children grew up, Jessie went back to being a nurse at the hospital and in the villages. In the villages, she would work with the sick women and children in the morning. When it was time to eat lunch, she and the Chinese Bible teachers would sing hymns and tell the Bible stories to the women and children. Sometimes, even the men would come and listen.

For many of the Chinese, this was the first time they had heard of Jesus Christ. Jessie was happy to tell them about God's love.

Jessie celebrates her eightieth birthday.

America and Japan went to war in 1941 when Jessie was sixty-four. The part of China where Wiley and Jessie lived had been taken over by Japanese soldiers.

The Japanese soldiers came to the Glass house and told them they were prisoners. They had to stop their missionary work. They could not leave the mission house. It was very hard not to be able to see their Chinese friends. Wiley and Jessie were glad that the children were grown and had moved far away—except for Lois, who was a missionary in a town nearby.

In the spring, Wiley and Jessie were sent to the city of Chefoo to get on a boat to come home to America. When they got to the boat, there was not enough room for everyone. They had to stay in Chefoo with friends. Soon, Lois was also sent to Chefoo. They were all still prisoners of the Japanese.

In the fall, everyone had to move closer together so the soldiers could watch them. Wiley and Jessie moved into a house with forty-two other people. Ten people were in the same bedroom. They had very little food.

The soldiers said they could have church on Sunday. Wiley was the preacher.

Finally, Wiley, Jessie, and Lois were put on an old ship to come to America. It rained almost every day. They were afraid the boat would sink. It was very hot on the boat. The food was not cooked very well. Sometimes, they did not have water. Jessie got sick.

They had to stay on this boat for a month until they got near India. Then the Japanese let them get on a boat to come across the ocean to America. On the new boat, they got mail from their family and friends. It was the first mail in two years.

The new boat sailed to Africa. Next it went around South Africa and into the Atlantic Ocean. Finally, after another month, the boat got to New York City. "Look, Jessie! Look, Lois! There is the Statue of Liberty!" Wiley cried.

Wiley and Jessie were glad to be home. They missed China, but they knew they could not go back because of the war. They moved to Texas but went to many churches all over America telling people about China. They tried to get people to give more money to missions and to go serve as missionaries themselves.

Wiley and Jessie were very happy spending time with their children and grandchildren. One happy time was a birthday party for Jessie when she was eighty years old.

"You know, God has been so good to me," Jessie said. "He sent me to China. He let me be a nurse for forty years. He gave me a husband I love. He gave me five children. He kept me safe. Best of all, he let me tell people who did not know Jesus that he died to save them from their sins. I am so glad God let me be a missionary. That is all I ever wanted to be."

Mr. and Mrs. Glass spend time with family.